THIS JOURNAL BELONGS TO

_____

DATE: /   /   S M T W TH F S

5 AM
6 AM
7 AM
8 AM
9 AM
10 AM
11 AM
12 PM
1 PM
2 PM
3 PM
4 PM
5 PM
6 PM
7 PM
8 PM
9 PM
10 PM
11 PM

NOTES & OTHER JAZZ

DAY ○

THE DAY'S #1 GOAL

3 TASKS THAT WILL HELP ME REACH MY GOAL

1.
2.
3.

EVENING ☾

HOW WELL DID I ACCOMPLISH MY GOAL TODAY?

FAILURE ○ 1   ○ 2   ○ 3   ○ 4   ○ 5   ○ 6   ○ 7   ○ 8   ○ 9   ○ 10 SUCCESS!

HERE'S A LITTLE SOMETHING I LEARNED TODAY

TODAY'S WINS

3 THINGS I'M THANKFUL FOR THIS EVENING

1.
2.
3.

DATE: / /   S M T W TH F S

- 5 AM
- 6 AM
- 7 AM
- 8 AM
- 9 AM
- 10 AM
- 11 AM
- 12 PM
- 1 PM
- 2 PM
- 3 PM
- 4 PM
- 5 PM
- 6 PM
- 7 PM
- 8 PM
- 9 PM
- 10 PM
- 11 PM

NOTES & OTHER JAZZ

DAY ○

THE DAY'S #1 GOAL

3 TASKS THAT WILL HELP ME REACH MY GOAL

1.
2.
3.

EVENING ☾

HOW WELL DID I ACCOMPLISH MY GOAL TODAY?

FAILURE ○ ○ ○ ○ ○ ○ ○ ○ ○ ○ SUCCESS!
        1 2 3 4 5 6 7 8 9 10

HERE'S A LITTLE SOMETHING I LEARNED TODAY

TODAY'S WINS

3 THINGS I'M THANKFUL FOR THIS EVENING

1.
2.
3.

DATE: / /   S M T W TH F S

- 5 AM
- 6 AM
- 7 AM
- 8 AM
- 9 AM
- 10 AM
- 11 AM
- 12 PM
- 1 PM
- 2 PM
- 3 PM
- 4 PM
- 5 PM
- 6 PM
- 7 PM
- 8 PM
- 9 PM
- 10 PM
- 11 PM

NOTES & OTHER JAZZ

DAY ○

THE DAY'S #1 GOAL

3 TASKS THAT WILL HELP ME REACH MY GOAL

1.
2.
3.

EVENING ☾

HOW WELL DID I ACCOMPLISH MY GOAL TODAY?

FAILURE ○ ○ ○ ○ ○ ○ ○ ○ ○ ○ SUCCESS!
       1 2 3 4 5 6 7 8 9 10

HERE'S A LITTLE SOMETHING I LEARNED TODAY

TODAY'S WINS

3 THINGS I'M THANKFUL FOR THIS EVENING

1.
2.
3.

DATE: / / S M T W TH F S

5 AM
6 AM
7 AM
8 AM
9 AM
10 AM
11 AM
12 PM
1 PM
2 PM
3 PM
4 PM
5 PM
6 PM
7 PM
8 PM
9 PM
10 PM
11 PM

NOTES & OTHER JAZZ

DAY ○

THE DAY'S #1 GOAL

3 TASKS THAT WILL HELP ME REACH MY GOAL

1.
2.
3.

EVENING ☾

HOW WELL DID I ACCOMPLISH MY GOAL TODAY?

FAILURE ○ ○ ○ ○ ○ ○ ○ ○ ○ ○ SUCCESS!
        1 2 3 4 5 6 7 8 9 10

HERE'S A LITTLE SOMETHING I LEARNED TODAY

TODAY'S WINS

3 THINGS I'M THANKFUL FOR THIS EVENING

1.
2.
3.

DATE: / /   S M T W TH F S

- 5 AM
- 6 AM
- 7 AM
- 8 AM
- 9 AM
- 10 AM
- 11 AM
- 12 PM
- 1 PM
- 2 PM
- 3 PM
- 4 PM
- 5 PM
- 6 PM
- 7 PM
- 8 PM
- 9 PM
- 10 PM
- 11 PM

NOTES & OTHER JAZZ

DAY ◯

THE DAY'S #1 GOAL

3 TASKS THAT WILL HELP ME REACH MY GOAL

1.
2.
3.

EVENING ☾

HOW WELL DID I ACCOMPLISH MY GOAL TODAY?

FAILURE ◯ ◯ ◯ ◯ ◯ ◯ ◯ ◯ ◯ ◯ SUCCESS!
       1 2 3 4 5 6 7 8 9 10

HERE'S A LITTLE SOMETHING I LEARNED TODAY

TODAY'S WINS

3 THINGS I'M THANKFUL FOR THIS EVENING

1.
2.
3.

DATE: / /   S M T W TH F S

5 AM
6 AM
7 AM
8 AM
9 AM
10 AM
11 AM
12 PM
1 PM
2 PM
3 PM
4 PM
5 PM
6 PM
7 PM
8 PM
9 PM
10 PM
11 PM

NOTES & OTHER JAZZ

DAY ○

THE DAY'S #1 GOAL

3 TASKS THAT WILL HELP ME REACH MY GOAL

1.
2.
3.

EVENING ☾

HOW WELL DID I ACCOMPLISH MY GOAL TODAY?

FAILURE ○ ○ ○ ○ ○ ○ ○ ○ ○ ○ SUCCESS!
       1 2 3 4 5 6 7 8 9 10

HERE'S A LITTLE SOMETHING I LEARNED TODAY

TODAY'S WINS

3 THINGS I'M THANKFUL FOR THIS EVENING

1.
2.
3.

DATE: / /   S M T W TH F S

5 AM
6 AM
7 AM
8 AM
9 AM
10 AM
11 AM
12 PM
1 PM
2 PM
3 PM
4 PM
5 PM
6 PM
7 PM
8 PM
9 PM
10 PM
11 PM

NOTES & OTHER JAZZ

DAY ○

THE DAY'S #1 GOAL

3 TASKS THAT WILL HELP ME REACH MY GOAL

1.
2.
3.

EVENING ☾

HOW WELL DID I ACCOMPLISH MY GOAL TODAY?

FAILURE ○ ○ ○ ○ ○ ○ ○ ○ ○ ○ SUCCESS!
        1 2 3 4 5 6 7 8 9 10

HERE'S A LITTLE SOMETHING I LEARNED TODAY

TODAY'S WINS

3 THINGS I'M THANKFUL FOR THIS EVENING

1.
2.
3.

DATE: /   /   S M T W TH F S

Time	
5 AM	
6 AM	
7 AM	
8 AM	
9 AM	
10 AM	
11 AM	
12 PM	
1 PM	
2 PM	
3 PM	
4 PM	
5 PM	
6 PM	
7 PM	
8 PM	
9 PM	
10 PM	
11 PM	

NOTES & OTHER JAZZ

DAY ○

THE DAY'S #1 GOAL

3 TASKS THAT WILL HELP ME REACH MY GOAL

1.
2.
3.

EVENING

HOW WELL DID I ACCOMPLISH MY GOAL TODAY?

FAILURE ○ 1 ○ 2 ○ 3 ○ 4 ○ 5 ○ 6 ○ 7 ○ 8 ○ 9 ○ 10 SUCCESS!

HERE'S A LITTLE SOMETHING I LEARNED TODAY

TODAY'S WINS

3 THINGS I'M THANKFUL FOR THIS EVENING

1.
2.
3.

DATE: / /   S M T W TH F S

5 AM
6 AM
7 AM
8 AM
9 AM
10 AM
11 AM
12 PM
1 PM
2 PM
3 PM
4 PM
5 PM
6 PM
7 PM
8 PM
9 PM
10 PM
11 PM

NOTES & OTHER JAZZ

DAY ◯

THE DAY'S #1 GOAL

3 TASKS THAT WILL HELP ME REACH MY GOAL

1.
2.
3.

EVENING ☾

HOW WELL DID I ACCOMPLISH MY GOAL TODAY?

FAILURE ◯ ◯ ◯ ◯ ◯ ◯ ◯ ◯ ◯ ◯ SUCCESS!
       1 2 3 4 5 6 7 8 9 10

HERE'S A LITTLE SOMETHING I LEARNED TODAY

TODAY'S WINS

3 THINGS I'M THANKFUL FOR THIS EVENING

1.
2.
3.

DATE: /   /   S M T W TH F S

- 5 AM
- 6 AM
- 7 AM
- 8 AM
- 9 AM
- 10 AM
- 11 AM
- 12 PM
- 1 PM
- 2 PM
- 3 PM
- 4 PM
- 5 PM
- 6 PM
- 7 PM
- 8 PM
- 9 PM
- 10 PM
- 11 PM

NOTES & OTHER JAZZ

DAY ○

THE DAY'S #1 GOAL

3 TASKS THAT WILL HELP ME REACH MY GOAL

1.
2.
3.

EVENING

HOW WELL DID I ACCOMPLISH MY GOAL TODAY?

FAILURE ○ 1 ○ 2 ○ 3 ○ 4 ○ 5 ○ 6 ○ 7 ○ 8 ○ 9 ○ 10 SUCCESS!

HERE'S A LITTLE SOMETHING I LEARNED TODAY

TODAY'S WINS

3 THINGS I'M THANKFUL FOR THIS EVENING

1.
2.
3.

DATE: / /   S M T W TH F S

5 AM

6 AM

7 AM

8 AM

9 AM

10 AM

11 AM

12 PM

1 PM

2 PM

3 PM

4 PM

5 PM

6 PM

7 PM

8 PM

9 PM

10 PM

11 PM

NOTES & OTHER JAZZ

DAY ○

THE DAY'S #1 GOAL

3 TASKS THAT WILL HELP ME REACH MY GOAL

1.
2.
3.

EVENING ☾

HOW WELL DID I ACCOMPLISH MY GOAL TODAY?

FAILURE ○ ○ ○ ○ ○ ○ ○ ○ ○ ○ SUCCESS!
       1 2 3 4 5 6 7 8 9 10

HERE'S A LITTLE SOMETHING I LEARNED TODAY

TODAY'S WINS

3 THINGS I'M THANKFUL FOR THIS EVENING

1.
2.
3.

DATE: / /   S M T W TH F S

5 AM
6 AM
7 AM
8 AM
9 AM
10 AM
11 AM
12 PM
1 PM
2 PM
3 PM
4 PM
5 PM
6 PM
7 PM
8 PM
9 PM
10 PM
11 PM

NOTES & OTHER JAZZ

DAY ○

THE DAY'S #1 GOAL

3 TASKS THAT WILL HELP ME REACH MY GOAL

1.
2.
3.

EVENING ☾

HOW WELL DID I ACCOMPLISH MY GOAL TODAY?

FAILURE ○ ○ ○ ○ ○ ○ ○ ○ ○ ○ SUCCESS!
         1 2 3 4 5 6 7 8 9 10

HERE'S A LITTLE SOMETHING I LEARNED TODAY

TODAY'S WINS

3 THINGS I'M THANKFUL FOR THIS EVENING

1.
2.
3.

DATE: /   /   S M T W TH F S

- 5 AM
- 6 AM
- 7 AM
- 8 AM
- 9 AM
- 10 AM
- 11 AM
- 12 PM
- 1 PM
- 2 PM
- 3 PM
- 4 PM
- 5 PM
- 6 PM
- 7 PM
- 8 PM
- 9 PM
- 10 PM
- 11 PM

NOTES & OTHER JAZZ

DAY ○

THE DAY'S #1 GOAL

3 TASKS THAT WILL HELP ME REACH MY GOAL

1.
2.
3.

EVENING ☾

HOW WELL DID I ACCOMPLISH MY GOAL TODAY?

FAILURE ○ ○ ○ ○ ○ ○ ○ ○ ○ ○ SUCCESS!
        1   2   3   4   5   6   7   8   9   10

HERE'S A LITTLE SOMETHING I LEARNED TODAY

TODAY'S WINS

3 THINGS I'M THANKFUL FOR THIS EVENING

1.
2.
3.

DATE: / /   S M T W TH F S

5 AM
6 AM
7 AM
8 AM
9 AM
10 AM
11 AM
12 PM
1 PM
2 PM
3 PM
4 PM
5 PM
6 PM
7 PM
8 PM
9 PM
10 PM
11 PM

NOTES & OTHER JAZZ

DAY ○

THE DAY'S #1 GOAL

3 TASKS THAT WILL HELP ME REACH MY GOAL

1.
2.
3.

EVENING ☾

HOW WELL DID I ACCOMPLISH MY GOAL TODAY?

FAILURE ○ 1 ○ 2 ○ 3 ○ 4 ○ 5 ○ 6 ○ 7 ○ 8 ○ 9 ○ 10 SUCCESS!

HERE'S A LITTLE SOMETHING I LEARNED TODAY

TODAY'S WINS

3 THINGS I'M THANKFUL FOR THIS EVENING

1.
2.
3.

DATE: / /   S M T W TH F S

- 5 AM
- 6 AM
- 7 AM
- 8 AM
- 9 AM
- 10 AM
- 11 AM
- 12 PM
- 1 PM
- 2 PM
- 3 PM
- 4 PM
- 5 PM
- 6 PM
- 7 PM
- 8 PM
- 9 PM
- 10 PM
- 11 PM

NOTES & OTHER JAZZ

DAY ○

THE DAY'S #1 GOAL

3 TASKS THAT WILL HELP ME REACH MY GOAL

1.
2.
3.

EVENING ☾

HOW WELL DID I ACCOMPLISH MY GOAL TODAY?

FAILURE ○ 1 ○ 2 ○ 3 ○ 4 ○ 5 ○ 6 ○ 7 ○ 8 ○ 9 ○ 10 SUCCESS!

HERE'S A LITTLE SOMETHING I LEARNED TODAY

TODAY'S WINS

3 THINGS I'M THANKFUL FOR THIS EVENING

1.
2.
3.

DATE: /   /   S M T W TH F S

Time		NOTES & OTHER JAZZ
5 AM		
6 AM		
7 AM		
8 AM		
9 AM		
10 AM		
11 AM		
12 PM		
1 PM		
2 PM		
3 PM		
4 PM		
5 PM		
6 PM		
7 PM		
8 PM		
9 PM		
10 PM		
11 PM		

DAY ○

THE DAY'S #1 GOAL

3 TASKS THAT WILL HELP ME REACH MY GOAL

1.
2.
3.

EVENING ☾

HOW WELL DID I ACCOMPLISH MY GOAL TODAY?

FAILURE ○ ○ ○ ○ ○ ○ ○ ○ ○ ○ SUCCESS!
       1 2 3 4 5 6 7 8 9 10

HERE'S A LITTLE SOMETHING I LEARNED TODAY

TODAY'S WINS

3 THINGS I'M THANKFUL FOR THIS EVENING

1.
2.
3.

DATE: /   /   S M T W TH F S

5 AM
6 AM
7 AM
8 AM
9 AM
10 AM
11 AM
12 PM
1 PM
2 PM
3 PM
4 PM
5 PM
6 PM
7 PM
8 PM
9 PM
10 PM
11 PM

NOTES & OTHER JAZZ

DAY 🔾

THE DAY'S #1 GOAL

3 TASKS THAT WILL HELP ME REACH MY GOAL

1.
2.
3.

EVENING ☾

HOW WELL DID I ACCOMPLISH MY GOAL TODAY?

FAILURE 1 2 3 4 5 6 7 8 9 10 SUCCESS!

HERE'S A LITTLE SOMETHING I LEARNED TODAY

TODAY'S WINS

3 THINGS I'M THANKFUL FOR THIS EVENING

1.
2.
3.

DATE: /   /   S M T W TH F S

- 5 AM
- 6 AM
- 7 AM
- 8 AM
- 9 AM
- 10 AM
- 11 AM
- 12 PM
- 1 PM
- 2 PM
- 3 PM
- 4 PM
- 5 PM
- 6 PM
- 7 PM
- 8 PM
- 9 PM
- 10 PM
- 11 PM

NOTES & OTHER JAZZ

DAY ○

THE DAY'S #1 GOAL

3 TASKS THAT WILL HELP ME REACH MY GOAL

1.
2.
3.

EVENING ☾

HOW WELL DID I ACCOMPLISH MY GOAL TODAY?

FAILURE ○ 1   ○ 2   ○ 3   ○ 4   ○ 5   ○ 6   ○ 7   ○ 8   ○ 9   ○ 10   SUCCESS!

HERE'S A LITTLE SOMETHING I LEARNED TODAY

TODAY'S WINS

3 THINGS I'M THANKFUL FOR THIS EVENING

1.
2.
3.

DATE: /   /   S M T W TH F S

- 5 AM
- 6 AM
- 7 AM
- 8 AM
- 9 AM
- 10 AM
- 11 AM
- 12 PM
- 1 PM
- 2 PM
- 3 PM
- 4 PM
- 5 PM
- 6 PM
- 7 PM
- 8 PM
- 9 PM
- 10 PM
- 11 PM

NOTES & OTHER JAZZ

DAY ○

THE DAY'S #1 GOAL

3 TASKS THAT WILL HELP ME REACH MY GOAL

1.
2.
3.

EVENING ☾

HOW WELL DID I ACCOMPLISH MY GOAL TODAY?

FAILURE ○ ○ ○ ○ ○ ○ ○ ○ ○ ○ SUCCESS!
          1 2 3 4 5 6 7 8 9 10

HERE'S A LITTLE SOMETHING I LEARNED TODAY

TODAY'S WINS

3 THINGS I'M THANKFUL FOR THIS EVENING

1.
2.
3.

DATE: / /   S M T W TH F S

Time		NOTES & OTHER JAZZ
5 AM		
6 AM		
7 AM		
8 AM		
9 AM		
10 AM		
11 AM		
12 PM		
1 PM		
2 PM		
3 PM		
4 PM		
5 PM		
6 PM		
7 PM		
8 PM		
9 PM		
10 PM		
11 PM		

DAY ○

THE DAY'S #1 GOAL

3 TASKS THAT WILL HELP ME REACH MY GOAL

1.
2.
3.

EVENING ☾

HOW WELL DID I ACCOMPLISH MY GOAL TODAY?

FAILURE ○ 1   ○ 2   ○ 3   ○ 4   ○ 5   ○ 6   ○ 7   ○ 8   ○ 9   ○ 10 SUCCESS!

HERE'S A LITTLE SOMETHING I LEARNED TODAY

TODAY'S WINS

3 THINGS I'M THANKFUL FOR THIS EVENING

1.
2.
3.

DATE: / /   S M T W TH F S

- 5 AM
- 6 AM
- 7 AM
- 8 AM
- 9 AM
- 10 AM
- 11 AM
- 12 PM
- 1 PM
- 2 PM
- 3 PM
- 4 PM
- 5 PM
- 6 PM
- 7 PM
- 8 PM
- 9 PM
- 10 PM
- 11 PM

NOTES & OTHER JAZZ

DAY ○

THE DAY'S #1 GOAL

3 TASKS THAT WILL HELP ME REACH MY GOAL

1.
2.
3.

EVENING ☾

HOW WELL DID I ACCOMPLISH MY GOAL TODAY?

FAILURE ○ 1 ○ 2 ○ 3 ○ 4 ○ 5 ○ 6 ○ 7 ○ 8 ○ 9 ○ 10 SUCCESS!

HERE'S A LITTLE SOMETHING I LEARNED TODAY

TODAY'S WINS

3 THINGS I'M THANKFUL FOR THIS EVENING

1.
2.
3.

DATE: /   /   S M T W TH F S

- 5 AM
- 6 AM
- 7 AM
- 8 AM
- 9 AM
- 10 AM
- 11 AM
- 12 PM
- 1 PM
- 2 PM
- 3 PM
- 4 PM
- 5 PM
- 6 PM
- 7 PM
- 8 PM
- 9 PM
- 10 PM
- 11 PM

NOTES & OTHER JAZZ

DAY ○

THE DAY'S #1 GOAL

3 TASKS THAT WILL HELP ME REACH MY GOAL

1.
2.
3.

EVENING ☾

HOW WELL DID I ACCOMPLISH MY GOAL TODAY?

FAILURE ○ 1   ○ 2   ○ 3   ○ 4   ○ 5   ○ 6   ○ 7   ○ 8   ○ 9   ○ 10   SUCCESS!

HERE'S A LITTLE SOMETHING I LEARNED TODAY

TODAY'S WINS

3 THINGS I'M THANKFUL FOR THIS EVENING

1.
2.
3.

DATE: / /   S M T W TH F S

5 AM
6 AM
7 AM
8 AM
9 AM
10 AM
11 AM
12 PM
1 PM
2 PM
3 PM
4 PM
5 PM
6 PM
7 PM
8 PM
9 PM
10 PM
11 PM

NOTES & OTHER JAZZ

DAY ○

THE DAY'S #1 GOAL

3 TASKS THAT WILL HELP ME REACH MY GOAL

1.
2.
3.

EVENING ☾

HOW WELL DID I ACCOMPLISH MY GOAL TODAY?

FAILURE ○ 1 ○ 2 ○ 3 ○ 4 ○ 5 ○ 6 ○ 7 ○ 8 ○ 9 ○ 10 SUCCESS!

HERE'S A LITTLE SOMETHING I LEARNED TODAY

TODAY'S WINS

3 THINGS I'M THANKFUL FOR THIS EVENING

1.
2.
3.

DATE: / /   S M T W TH F S

5 AM
6 AM
7 AM
8 AM
9 AM
10 AM
11 AM
12 PM
1 PM
2 PM
3 PM
4 PM
5 PM
6 PM
7 PM
8 PM
9 PM
10 PM
11 PM

NOTES & OTHER JAZZ

DAY ○

THE DAY'S #1 GOAL

3 TASKS THAT WILL HELP ME REACH MY GOAL

1.
2.
3.

EVENING ☾

HOW WELL DID I ACCOMPLISH MY GOAL TODAY?

FAILURE ○ ○ ○ ○ ○ ○ ○ ○ ○ ○ SUCCESS!
       1 2 3 4 5 6 7 8 9 10

HERE'S A LITTLE SOMETHING I LEARNED TODAY

TODAY'S WINS

3 THINGS I'M THANKFUL FOR THIS EVENING

1.
2.
3.

DATE: / /   S M T W TH F S

Time	
5 AM	
6 AM	
7 AM	
8 AM	
9 AM	
10 AM	
11 AM	
12 PM	
1 PM	
2 PM	
3 PM	
4 PM	
5 PM	
6 PM	
7 PM	
8 PM	
9 PM	
10 PM	
11 PM	

NOTES & OTHER JAZZ

DAY ○

THE DAY'S #1 GOAL

3 TASKS THAT WILL HELP ME REACH MY GOAL

1.
2.
3.

EVENING ☾

HOW WELL DID I ACCOMPLISH MY GOAL TODAY?

FAILURE ○ ○ ○ ○ ○ ○ ○ ○ ○ ○ SUCCESS!
      1 2 3 4 5 6 7 8 9 10

HERE'S A LITTLE SOMETHING I LEARNED TODAY

TODAY'S WINS

3 THINGS I'M THANKFUL FOR THIS EVENING

1.
2.
3.

DATE: /   /   S M T W TH F S

- 5 AM
- 6 AM
- 7 AM
- 8 AM
- 9 AM
- 10 AM
- 11 AM
- 12 PM
- 1 PM
- 2 PM
- 3 PM
- 4 PM
- 5 PM
- 6 PM
- 7 PM
- 8 PM
- 9 PM
- 10 PM
- 11 PM

NOTES & OTHER JAZZ

DAY ○

THE DAY'S #1 GOAL

3 TASKS THAT WILL HELP ME REACH MY GOAL

1.
2.
3.

EVENING ☾

HOW WELL DID I ACCOMPLISH MY GOAL TODAY?

FAILURE ○ 1   ○ 2   ○ 3   ○ 4   ○ 5   ○ 6   ○ 7   ○ 8   ○ 9   ○ 10 SUCCESS!

HERE'S A LITTLE SOMETHING I LEARNED TODAY

TODAY'S WINS

3 THINGS I'M THANKFUL FOR THIS EVENING

1.
2.
3.

DATE: / /   S M T W TH F S

5 AM
6 AM
7 AM
8 AM
9 AM
10 AM
11 AM
12 PM
1 PM
2 PM
3 PM
4 PM
5 PM
6 PM
7 PM
8 PM
9 PM
10 PM
11 PM

NOTES & OTHER JAZZ

DAY ○

THE DAY'S #1 GOAL

3 TASKS THAT WILL HELP ME REACH MY GOAL

1.
2.
3.

EVENING ☾

HOW WELL DID I ACCOMPLISH MY GOAL TODAY?

FAILURE ○ ○ ○ ○ ○ ○ ○ ○ ○ ○ SUCCESS!
         1 2 3 4 5 6 7 8 9 10

HERE'S A LITTLE SOMETHING I LEARNED TODAY

TODAY'S WINS

3 THINGS I'M THANKFUL FOR THIS EVENING

1.
2.
3.

DATE: / /   S M T W TH F S

- 5 AM
- 6 AM
- 7 AM
- 8 AM
- 9 AM
- 10 AM
- 11 AM
- 12 PM
- 1 PM
- 2 PM
- 3 PM
- 4 PM
- 5 PM
- 6 PM
- 7 PM
- 8 PM
- 9 PM
- 10 PM
- 11 PM

NOTES & OTHER JAZZ

DAY ○

THE DAY'S #1 GOAL

3 TASKS THAT WILL HELP ME REACH MY GOAL

1.
2.
3.

EVENING ☾

HOW WELL DID I ACCOMPLISH MY GOAL TODAY?

FAILURE ○ ○ ○ ○ ○ ○ ○ ○ ○ ○ SUCCESS!
        1 2 3 4 5 6 7 8 9 10

HERE'S A LITTLE SOMETHING I LEARNED TODAY

TODAY'S WINS

3 THINGS I'M THANKFUL FOR THIS EVENING

1.
2.
3.

DATE: / /   S M T W TH F S

- 5 AM
- 6 AM
- 7 AM
- 8 AM
- 9 AM
- 10 AM
- 11 AM
- 12 PM
- 1 PM
- 2 PM
- 3 PM
- 4 PM
- 5 PM
- 6 PM
- 7 PM
- 8 PM
- 9 PM
- 10 PM
- 11 PM

NOTES & OTHER JAZZ

DAY ○

THE DAY'S #1 GOAL

3 TASKS THAT WILL HELP ME REACH MY GOAL

1.
2.
3.

EVENING ☾

HOW WELL DID I ACCOMPLISH MY GOAL TODAY?

FAILURE ○ 1   ○ 2   ○ 3   ○ 4   ○ 5   ○ 6   ○ 7   ○ 8   ○ 9   ○ 10   SUCCESS!

HERE'S A LITTLE SOMETHING I LEARNED TODAY

TODAY'S WINS

3 THINGS I'M THANKFUL FOR THIS EVENING

1.
2.
3.

DATE: /   /   S M T W TH F S

Time	
5 AM	
6 AM	
7 AM	
8 AM	
9 AM	
10 AM	
11 AM	
12 PM	
1 PM	
2 PM	
3 PM	
4 PM	
5 PM	
6 PM	
7 PM	
8 PM	
9 PM	
10 PM	
11 PM	

NOTES & OTHER JAZZ

DAY ○

THE DAY'S #1 GOAL

3 TASKS THAT WILL HELP ME REACH MY GOAL

1.
2.
3.

EVENING ☾

HOW WELL DID I ACCOMPLISH MY GOAL TODAY?

FAILURE ○ ○ ○ ○ ○ ○ ○ ○ ○ ○ SUCCESS!
      1 2 3 4 5 6 7 8 9 10

HERE'S A LITTLE SOMETHING I LEARNED TODAY

TODAY'S WINS

3 THINGS I'M THANKFUL FOR THIS EVENING

1.
2.
3.

DATE: / /   S M T W TH F S

- 5 AM
- 6 AM
- 7 AM
- 8 AM
- 9 AM
- 10 AM
- 11 AM
- 12 PM
- 1 PM
- 2 PM
- 3 PM
- 4 PM
- 5 PM
- 6 PM
- 7 PM
- 8 PM
- 9 PM
- 10 PM
- 11 PM

NOTES & OTHER JAZZ

DAY ○

THE DAY'S #1 GOAL

3 TASKS THAT WILL HELP ME REACH MY GOAL

1.
2.
3.

EVENING ☾

HOW WELL DID I ACCOMPLISH MY GOAL TODAY?

FAILURE ○ 1 ○ 2 ○ 3 ○ 4 ○ 5 ○ 6 ○ 7 ○ 8 ○ 9 ○ 10 SUCCESS!

HERE'S A LITTLE SOMETHING I LEARNED TODAY

TODAY'S WINS

3 THINGS I'M THANKFUL FOR THIS EVENING

1.
2.
3.

DATE: / /   S M T W TH F S

- 5 AM
- 6 AM
- 7 AM
- 8 AM
- 9 AM
- 10 AM
- 11 AM
- 12 PM
- 1 PM
- 2 PM
- 3 PM
- 4 PM
- 5 PM
- 6 PM
- 7 PM
- 8 PM
- 9 PM
- 10 PM
- 11 PM

NOTES & OTHER JAZZ

DAY ○

THE DAY'S #1 GOAL

3 TASKS THAT WILL HELP ME REACH MY GOAL

1.
2.
3.

EVENING ☾

HOW WELL DID I ACCOMPLISH MY GOAL TODAY?

FAILURE ○ ○ ○ ○ ○ ○ ○ ○ ○ ○ SUCCESS!
        1 2 3 4 5 6 7 8 9 10

HERE'S A LITTLE SOMETHING I LEARNED TODAY

TODAY'S WINS

3 THINGS I'M THANKFUL FOR THIS EVENING

1.
2.
3.

DATE: / /   S M T W TH F S

- 5 AM
- 6 AM
- 7 AM
- 8 AM
- 9 AM
- 10 AM
- 11 AM
- 12 PM
- 1 PM
- 2 PM
- 3 PM
- 4 PM
- 5 PM
- 6 PM
- 7 PM
- 8 PM
- 9 PM
- 10 PM
- 11 PM

NOTES & OTHER JAZZ

DAY ○

THE DAY'S #1 GOAL

3 TASKS THAT WILL HELP ME REACH MY GOAL

1.
2.
3.

EVENING ☾

HOW WELL DID I ACCOMPLISH MY GOAL TODAY?

FAILURE ○ ○ ○ ○ ○ ○ ○ ○ ○ ○ SUCCESS!
        1 2 3 4 5 6 7 8 9 10

HERE'S A LITTLE SOMETHING I LEARNED TODAY

TODAY'S WINS

3 THINGS I'M THANKFUL FOR THIS EVENING

1.
2.
3.

DATE: /   /   S M T W TH F S

Time	
5 AM	
6 AM	
7 AM	
8 AM	
9 AM	
10 AM	
11 AM	
12 PM	
1 PM	
2 PM	
3 PM	
4 PM	
5 PM	
6 PM	
7 PM	
8 PM	
9 PM	
10 PM	
11 PM	

NOTES & OTHER JAZZ

DAY ○

THE DAY'S #1 GOAL

3 TASKS THAT WILL HELP ME REACH MY GOAL

1.
2.
3.

EVENING ☾

HOW WELL DID I ACCOMPLISH MY GOAL TODAY?

FAILURE ○ 1 ○ 2 ○ 3 ○ 4 ○ 5 ○ 6 ○ 7 ○ 8 ○ 9 ○ 10 SUCCESS!

HERE'S A LITTLE SOMETHING I LEARNED TODAY

TODAY'S WINS

3 THINGS I'M THANKFUL FOR THIS EVENING

1.
2.
3.

DATE: / /   S M T W TH F S

5 AM
6 AM
7 AM
8 AM
9 AM
10 AM
11 AM
12 PM
1 PM
2 PM
3 PM
4 PM
5 PM
6 PM
7 PM
8 PM
9 PM
10 PM
11 PM

NOTES & OTHER JAZZ

DAY ○

THE DAY'S #1 GOAL

3 TASKS THAT WILL HELP ME REACH MY GOAL

1.
2.
3.

EVENING ☾

HOW WELL DID I ACCOMPLISH MY GOAL TODAY?

FAILURE ○ ○ ○ ○ ○ ○ ○ ○ ○ ○ SUCCESS!
         1 2 3 4 5 6 7 8 9 10

HERE'S A LITTLE SOMETHING I LEARNED TODAY

TODAY'S WINS

3 THINGS I'M THANKFUL FOR THIS EVENING

1.
2.
3.

DATE: /   /   S M T W TH F S

Time		Notes & Other Jazz
5 AM		
6 AM		
7 AM		
8 AM		
9 AM		
10 AM		
11 AM		
12 PM		
1 PM		
2 PM		
3 PM		
4 PM		
5 PM		
6 PM		
7 PM		
8 PM		
9 PM		
10 PM		
11 PM		

DAY ○

THE DAY'S #1 GOAL

3 TASKS THAT WILL HELP ME REACH MY GOAL

1.
2.
3.

EVENING ☾

HOW WELL DID I ACCOMPLISH MY GOAL TODAY?

FAILURE ○ 1 ○ 2 ○ 3 ○ 4 ○ 5 ○ 6 ○ 7 ○ 8 ○ 9 ○ 10 SUCCESS!

HERE'S A LITTLE SOMETHING I LEARNED TODAY

TODAY'S WINS

3 THINGS I'M THANKFUL FOR THIS EVENING

1.
2.
3.

DATE: / /   S M T W TH F S

- 5 AM
- 6 AM
- 7 AM
- 8 AM
- 9 AM
- 10 AM
- 11 AM
- 12 PM
- 1 PM
- 2 PM
- 3 PM
- 4 PM
- 5 PM
- 6 PM
- 7 PM
- 8 PM
- 9 PM
- 10 PM
- 11 PM

NOTES & OTHER JAZZ

DAY ○

THE DAY'S #1 GOAL

3 TASKS THAT WILL HELP ME REACH MY GOAL

1.
2.
3.

EVENING ☾

HOW WELL DID I ACCOMPLISH MY GOAL TODAY?

FAILURE ○ 1 ○ 2 ○ 3 ○ 4 ○ 5 ○ 6 ○ 7 ○ 8 ○ 9 ○ 10 SUCCESS!

HERE'S A LITTLE SOMETHING I LEARNED TODAY

TODAY'S WINS

3 THINGS I'M THANKFUL FOR THIS EVENING

1.
2.
3.

DATE: / /   S M T W TH F S

5 AM
6 AM
7 AM
8 AM
9 AM
10 AM
11 AM
12 PM
1 PM
2 PM
3 PM
4 PM
5 PM
6 PM
7 PM
8 PM
9 PM
10 PM
11 PM

NOTES & OTHER JAZZ

DAY ○

THE DAY'S #1 GOAL

3 TASKS THAT WILL HELP ME REACH MY GOAL

1.
2.
3.

EVENING ☾

HOW WELL DID I ACCOMPLISH MY GOAL TODAY?

FAILURE ○ 1 ○ 2 ○ 3 ○ 4 ○ 5 ○ 6 ○ 7 ○ 8 ○ 9 ○ 10 SUCCESS!

HERE'S A LITTLE SOMETHING I LEARNED TODAY

TODAY'S WINS

3 THINGS I'M THANKFUL FOR THIS EVENING

1.
2.
3.

DATE: /   /   S M T W TH F S

NOTES & OTHER JAZZ

- 5 AM
- 6 AM
- 7 AM
- 8 AM
- 9 AM
- 10 AM
- 11 AM
- 12 PM
- 1 PM
- 2 PM
- 3 PM
- 4 PM
- 5 PM
- 6 PM
- 7 PM
- 8 PM
- 9 PM
- 10 PM
- 11 PM

DAY ○

THE DAY'S #1 GOAL

3 TASKS THAT WILL HELP ME REACH MY GOAL

1.
2.
3.

EVENING ☾

HOW WELL DID I ACCOMPLISH MY GOAL TODAY?

FAILURE ○ ○ ○ ○ ○ ○ ○ ○ ○ ○ SUCCESS!
         1 2 3 4 5 6 7 8 9 10

HERE'S A LITTLE SOMETHING I LEARNED TODAY

TODAY'S WINS

3 THINGS I'M THANKFUL FOR THIS EVENING

1.
2.
3.

DATE: /   /   S M T W TH F S

Time		Notes & Other Jazz
5 AM		
6 AM		
7 AM		
8 AM		
9 AM		
10 AM		
11 AM		
12 PM		
1 PM		
2 PM		
3 PM		
4 PM		
5 PM		
6 PM		
7 PM		
8 PM		
9 PM		
10 PM		
11 PM		

DAY ○

THE DAY'S #1 GOAL

3 TASKS THAT WILL HELP ME REACH MY GOAL

1. ....
2. ....
3. ....

EVENING ☾

HOW WELL DID I ACCOMPLISH MY GOAL TODAY?

FAILURE ○ 1   ○ 2   ○ 3   ○ 4   ○ 5   ○ 6   ○ 7   ○ 8   ○ 9   ○ 10   SUCCESS!

HERE'S A LITTLE SOMETHING I LEARNED TODAY

TODAY'S WINS

3 THINGS I'M THANKFUL FOR THIS EVENING

1. ....
2. ....
3. ....

DATE: /   /   S M T W TH F S

5 AM ....

NOTES & OTHER JAZZ

6 AM ....

7 AM ....

8 AM ....

9 AM ....

10 AM ....

11 AM ....

12 PM ....

1 PM ....

2 PM ....

3 PM ....

4 PM ....

5 PM ....

6 PM ....

7 PM ....

8 PM ....

9 PM ....

10 PM ....

11 PM ....

DAY ○

THE DAY'S #1 GOAL

3 TASKS THAT WILL HELP ME REACH MY GOAL

1.
2.
3.

EVENING ☾

HOW WELL DID I ACCOMPLISH MY GOAL TODAY?

FAILURE ○ ○ ○ ○ ○ ○ ○ ○ ○ ○ SUCCESS!
         1 2 3 4 5 6 7 8 9 10

HERE'S A LITTLE SOMETHING I LEARNED TODAY

TODAY'S WINS

3 THINGS I'M THANKFUL FOR THIS EVENING

1.
2.
3.

DATE: /   /   S M T W TH F S

5 AM
6 AM
7 AM
8 AM
9 AM
10 AM
11 AM
12 PM
1 PM
2 PM
3 PM
4 PM
5 PM
6 PM
7 PM
8 PM
9 PM
10 PM
11 PM

NOTES & OTHER JAZZ

DAY ○

THE DAY'S #1 GOAL

3 TASKS THAT WILL HELP ME REACH MY GOAL

1.
2.
3.

EVENING ☾

HOW WELL DID I ACCOMPLISH MY GOAL TODAY?

FAILURE ○ ○ ○ ○ ○ ○ ○ ○ ○ ○ SUCCESS!
       1 2 3 4 5 6 7 8 9 10

HERE'S A LITTLE SOMETHING I LEARNED TODAY

TODAY'S WINS

3 THINGS I'M THANKFUL FOR THIS EVENING

1.
2.
3.

DATE: /   /   S M T W TH F S

5 AM
6 AM
7 AM
8 AM
9 AM
10 AM
11 AM
12 PM
1 PM
2 PM
3 PM
4 PM
5 PM
6 PM
7 PM
8 PM
9 PM
10 PM
11 PM

NOTES & OTHER JAZZ

DAY ○

THE DAY'S #1 GOAL

3 TASKS THAT WILL HELP ME REACH MY GOAL

1.
2.
3.

EVENING ☾

HOW WELL DID I ACCOMPLISH MY GOAL TODAY?

FAILURE ○ ○ ○ ○ ○ ○ ○ ○ ○ ○ SUCCESS!
         1 2 3 4 5 6 7 8 9 10

HERE'S A LITTLE SOMETHING I LEARNED TODAY

TODAY'S WINS

3 THINGS I'M THANKFUL FOR THIS EVENING

1.
2.
3.

DATE: /   /   S M T W TH F S

- 5 AM
- 6 AM
- 7 AM
- 8 AM
- 9 AM
- 10 AM
- 11 AM
- 12 PM
- 1 PM
- 2 PM
- 3 PM
- 4 PM
- 5 PM
- 6 PM
- 7 PM
- 8 PM
- 9 PM
- 10 PM
- 11 PM

NOTES & OTHER JAZZ

DAY ○

THE DAY'S #1 GOAL

3 TASKS THAT WILL HELP ME REACH MY GOAL

1.
2.
3.

EVENING ☾

HOW WELL DID I ACCOMPLISH MY GOAL TODAY?

FAILURE ○ ○ ○ ○ ○ ○ ○ ○ ○ ○ SUCCESS!
        1 2 3 4 5 6 7 8 9 10

HERE'S A LITTLE SOMETHING I LEARNED TODAY

TODAY'S WINS

3 THINGS I'M THANKFUL FOR THIS EVENING

1.
2.
3.

DATE: / /   S M T W TH F S

- 5 AM
- 6 AM
- 7 AM
- 8 AM
- 9 AM
- 10 AM
- 11 AM
- 12 PM
- 1 PM
- 2 PM
- 3 PM
- 4 PM
- 5 PM
- 6 PM
- 7 PM
- 8 PM
- 9 PM
- 10 PM
- 11 PM

NOTES & OTHER JAZZ

DAY ◯

THE DAY'S #1 GOAL

3 TASKS THAT WILL HELP ME REACH MY GOAL

1.
2.
3.

EVENING ☾

HOW WELL DID I ACCOMPLISH MY GOAL TODAY?

FAILURE ◯ ◯ ◯ ◯ ◯ ◯ ◯ ◯ ◯ ◯ SUCCESS!
       1 2 3 4 5 6 7 8 9 10

HERE'S A LITTLE SOMETHING I LEARNED TODAY

TODAY'S WINS

3 THINGS I'M THANKFUL FOR THIS EVENING

1.
2.
3.

DATE: / /   S M T W TH F S

- 5 AM
- 6 AM
- 7 AM
- 8 AM
- 9 AM
- 10 AM
- 11 AM
- 12 PM
- 1 PM
- 2 PM
- 3 PM
- 4 PM
- 5 PM
- 6 PM
- 7 PM
- 8 PM
- 9 PM
- 10 PM
- 11 PM

NOTES & OTHER JAZZ

THE DAY'S #1 GOAL

DAY ○

3 TASKS THAT WILL HELP ME REACH MY GOAL

1.
2.
3.

EVENING ☾

HOW WELL DID I ACCOMPLISH MY GOAL TODAY?

FAILURE ○ ○ ○ ○ ○ ○ ○ ○ ○ ○ SUCCESS!
      1 2 3 4 5 6 7 8 9 10

HERE'S A LITTLE SOMETHING I LEARNED TODAY

TODAY'S WINS

3 THINGS I'M THANKFUL FOR THIS EVENING

1.
2.
3.

DATE: /   /   S M T W TH F S

5 AM
6 AM
7 AM
8 AM
9 AM
10 AM
11 AM
12 PM
1 PM
2 PM
3 PM
4 PM
5 PM
6 PM
7 PM
8 PM
9 PM
10 PM
11 PM

NOTES & OTHER JAZZ

DAY ○

THE DAY'S #1 GOAL

3 TASKS THAT WILL HELP ME REACH MY GOAL

1.
2.
3.

EVENING ☾

HOW WELL DID I ACCOMPLISH MY GOAL TODAY?

FAILURE ○ 1   ○ 2   ○ 3   ○ 4   ○ 5   ○ 6   ○ 7   ○ 8   ○ 9   ○ 10   SUCCESS!

HERE'S A LITTLE SOMETHING I LEARNED TODAY

TODAY'S WINS

3 THINGS I'M THANKFUL FOR THIS EVENING

1.
2.
3.

DATE: /   /   S M T W TH F S

Time	
5 AM	
6 AM	
7 AM	
8 AM	
9 AM	
10 AM	
11 AM	
12 PM	
1 PM	
2 PM	
3 PM	
4 PM	
5 PM	
6 PM	
7 PM	
8 PM	
9 PM	
10 PM	
11 PM	

NOTES & OTHER JAZZ

DAY ○

THE DAY'S #1 GOAL

3 TASKS THAT WILL HELP ME REACH MY GOAL

1.
2.
3.

EVENING ☾

HOW WELL DID I ACCOMPLISH MY GOAL TODAY?

FAILURE ○ ○ ○ ○ ○ ○ ○ ○ ○ ○ SUCCESS!
       1 2 3 4 5 6 7 8 9 10

HERE'S A LITTLE SOMETHING I LEARNED TODAY

TODAY'S WINS

3 THINGS I'M THANKFUL FOR THIS EVENING

1.
2.
3.

DATE: / /   S M T W TH F S

Time	
5 AM	
6 AM	
7 AM	
8 AM	
9 AM	
10 AM	
11 AM	
12 PM	
1 PM	
2 PM	
3 PM	
4 PM	
5 PM	
6 PM	
7 PM	
8 PM	
9 PM	
10 PM	
11 PM	

NOTES & OTHER JAZZ

DAY ○

THE DAY'S #1 GOAL

3 TASKS THAT WILL HELP ME REACH MY GOAL

1.
2.
3.

EVENING ☾

HOW WELL DID I ACCOMPLISH MY GOAL TODAY?

FAILURE ○ ○ ○ ○ ○ ○ ○ ○ ○ ○ SUCCESS!
       1 2 3 4 5 6 7 8 9 10

HERE'S A LITTLE SOMETHING I LEARNED TODAY

TODAY'S WINS

3 THINGS I'M THANKFUL FOR THIS EVENING

1.
2.
3.

DATE: /   /   S M T W TH F S

5 AM
6 AM
7 AM
8 AM
9 AM
10 AM
11 AM
12 PM
1 PM
2 PM
3 PM
4 PM
5 PM
6 PM
7 PM
8 PM
9 PM
10 PM
11 PM

NOTES & OTHER JAZZ

DAY ○

THE DAY'S #1 GOAL

3 TASKS THAT WILL HELP ME REACH MY GOAL

1.
2.
3.

EVENING ☾

HOW WELL DID I ACCOMPLISH MY GOAL TODAY?

FAILURE ○ ○ ○ ○ ○ ○ ○ ○ ○ ○ SUCCESS!
1 2 3 4 5 6 7 8 9 10

HERE'S A LITTLE SOMETHING I LEARNED TODAY

TODAY'S WINS

3 THINGS I'M THANKFUL FOR THIS EVENING

1.
2.
3.

DATE: / /   S M T W TH F S

Time	
5 AM	
6 AM	
7 AM	
8 AM	
9 AM	
10 AM	
11 AM	
12 PM	
1 PM	
2 PM	
3 PM	
4 PM	
5 PM	
6 PM	
7 PM	
8 PM	
9 PM	
10 PM	
11 PM	

NOTES & OTHER JAZZ

DAY ○

THE DAY'S #1 GOAL

3 TASKS THAT WILL HELP ME REACH MY GOAL

1.
2.
3.

EVENING ☾

HOW WELL DID I ACCOMPLISH MY GOAL TODAY?

FAILURE ○ 1 ○ 2 ○ 3 ○ 4 ○ 5 ○ 6 ○ 7 ○ 8 ○ 9 ○ 10 SUCCESS!

HERE'S A LITTLE SOMETHING I LEARNED TODAY

TODAY'S WINS

3 THINGS I'M THANKFUL FOR THIS EVENING

1.
2.
3.

DATE: / /   S M T W TH F S

- 5 AM
- 6 AM
- 7 AM
- 8 AM
- 9 AM
- 10 AM
- 11 AM
- 12 PM
- 1 PM
- 2 PM
- 3 PM
- 4 PM
- 5 PM
- 6 PM
- 7 PM
- 8 PM
- 9 PM
- 10 PM
- 11 PM

NOTES & OTHER JAZZ

DAY ○

THE DAY'S #1 GOAL

3 TASKS THAT WILL HELP ME REACH MY GOAL

1.
2.
3.

EVENING ☾

HOW WELL DID I ACCOMPLISH MY GOAL TODAY?

FAILURE ○ ○ ○ ○ ○ ○ ○ ○ ○ ○ SUCCESS!
         1 2 3 4 5 6 7 8 9 10

HERE'S A LITTLE SOMETHING I LEARNED TODAY

TODAY'S WINS

3 THINGS I'M THANKFUL FOR THIS EVENING

1.
2.
3.

DATE: / /   S M T W TH F S

Time	
5 AM	
6 AM	
7 AM	
8 AM	
9 AM	
10 AM	
11 AM	
12 PM	
1 PM	
2 PM	
3 PM	
4 PM	
5 PM	
6 PM	
7 PM	
8 PM	
9 PM	
10 PM	
11 PM	

NOTES & OTHER JAZZ

DAY ○

THE DAY'S #1 GOAL

3 TASKS THAT WILL HELP ME REACH MY GOAL

1.
2.
3.

EVENING ☾

HOW WELL DID I ACCOMPLISH MY GOAL TODAY?

FAILURE ○ ○ ○ ○ ○ ○ ○ ○ ○ ○ SUCCESS!
        1   2   3   4   5   6   7   8   9   10

HERE'S A LITTLE SOMETHING I LEARNED TODAY

TODAY'S WINS

3 THINGS I'M THANKFUL FOR THIS EVENING

1.
2.
3.

DATE: / /   S M T W TH F S

5 AM

6 AM

7 AM

8 AM

9 AM

10 AM

11 AM

12 PM

1 PM

2 PM

3 PM

4 PM

5 PM

6 PM

7 PM

8 PM

9 PM

10 PM

11 PM

NOTES & OTHER JAZZ

DAY ◯

THE DAY'S #1 GOAL

3 TASKS THAT WILL HELP ME REACH MY GOAL

1.
2.
3.

EVENING ☾

HOW WELL DID I ACCOMPLISH MY GOAL TODAY?

FAILURE ◯ ◯ ◯ ◯ ◯ ◯ ◯ ◯ ◯ ◯ SUCCESS!
       1 2 3 4 5 6 7 8 9 10

HERE'S A LITTLE SOMETHING I LEARNED TODAY

TODAY'S WINS

3 THINGS I'M THANKFUL FOR THIS EVENING

1.
2.
3.

DATE: /   /   S M T W TH F S

5 AM
6 AM
7 AM
8 AM
9 AM
10 AM
11 AM
12 PM
1 PM
2 PM
3 PM
4 PM
5 PM
6 PM
7 PM
8 PM
9 PM
10 PM
11 PM

NOTES & OTHER JAZZ

DAY ○

THE DAY'S #1 GOAL

3 TASKS THAT WILL HELP ME REACH MY GOAL

1.
2.
3.

EVENING ☾

HOW WELL DID I ACCOMPLISH MY GOAL TODAY?

FAILURE ○ 1 ○ 2 ○ 3 ○ 4 ○ 5 ○ 6 ○ 7 ○ 8 ○ 9 ○ 10 SUCCESS!

HERE'S A LITTLE SOMETHING I LEARNED TODAY

TODAY'S WINS

3 THINGS I'M THANKFUL FOR THIS EVENING

1.
2.
3.

DATE: /   /   S M T W TH F S

5 AM ....

6 AM ....

7 AM ....

8 AM ....

9 AM ....

10 AM ....

11 AM ....

12 PM ....

1 PM ....

2 PM ....

3 PM ....

4 PM ....

5 PM ....

6 PM ....

7 PM ....

8 PM ....

9 PM ....

10 PM ....

11 PM ....

NOTES & OTHER JAZZ

DAY ○

THE DAY'S #1 GOAL

3 TASKS THAT WILL HELP ME REACH MY GOAL

1.
2.
3.

EVENING ☾

HOW WELL DID I ACCOMPLISH MY GOAL TODAY?

FAILURE ○ ○ ○ ○ ○ ○ ○ ○ ○ ○ SUCCESS!
         1 2 3 4 5 6 7 8 9 10

HERE'S A LITTLE SOMETHING I LEARNED TODAY

TODAY'S WINS

3 THINGS I'M THANKFUL FOR THIS EVENING

1.
2.
3.

DATE: /   /   S M T W TH F S

Time		Notes & Other Jazz
5 AM		
6 AM		
7 AM		
8 AM		
9 AM		
10 AM		
11 AM		
12 PM		
1 PM		
2 PM		
3 PM		
4 PM		
5 PM		
6 PM		
7 PM		
8 PM		
9 PM		
10 PM		
11 PM		

DAY ○

THE DAY'S #1 GOAL

3 TASKS THAT WILL HELP ME REACH MY GOAL

1.
2.
3.

EVENING ☾

HOW WELL DID I ACCOMPLISH MY GOAL TODAY?

FAILURE ○ ○ ○ ○ ○ ○ ○ ○ ○ ○ SUCCESS!
        1   2   3   4   5   6   7   8   9   10

HERE'S A LITTLE SOMETHING I LEARNED TODAY

TODAY'S WINS

3 THINGS I'M THANKFUL FOR THIS EVENING

1.
2.
3.

DATE: / /   S M T W TH F S

5 AM
6 AM
7 AM
8 AM
9 AM
10 AM
11 AM
12 PM
1 PM
2 PM
3 PM
4 PM
5 PM
6 PM
7 PM
8 PM
9 PM
10 PM
11 PM

NOTES & OTHER JAZZ

DAY ○

THE DAY'S #1 GOAL

3 TASKS THAT WILL HELP ME REACH MY GOAL

1.
2.
3.

EVENING ☾

HOW WELL DID I ACCOMPLISH MY GOAL TODAY?

FAILURE ○ ○ ○ ○ ○ ○ ○ ○ ○ ○ SUCCESS!
         1 2 3 4 5 6 7 8 9 10

HERE'S A LITTLE SOMETHING I LEARNED TODAY

TODAY'S WINS

3 THINGS I'M THANKFUL FOR THIS EVENING

1.
2.
3.

DATE: /   /   S M T W TH F S

5 AM

6 AM

7 AM

8 AM

9 AM

10 AM

11 AM

12 PM

1 PM

2 PM

3 PM

4 PM

5 PM

6 PM

7 PM

8 PM

9 PM

10 PM

11 PM

NOTES & OTHER JAZZ

DAY ○

THE DAY'S #1 GOAL

3 TASKS THAT WILL HELP ME REACH MY GOAL

1.
2.
3.

EVENING ☾

HOW WELL DID I ACCOMPLISH MY GOAL TODAY?

FAILURE ○ ○ ○ ○ ○ ○ ○ ○ ○ ○ SUCCESS!
         1 2 3 4 5 6 7 8 9 10

HERE'S A LITTLE SOMETHING I LEARNED TODAY

TODAY'S WINS

3 THINGS I'M THANKFUL FOR THIS EVENING

1.
2.
3.

DATE: / /   S M T W TH F S

- 5 AM
- 6 AM
- 7 AM
- 8 AM
- 9 AM
- 10 AM
- 11 AM
- 12 PM
- 1 PM
- 2 PM
- 3 PM
- 4 PM
- 5 PM
- 6 PM
- 7 PM
- 8 PM
- 9 PM
- 10 PM
- 11 PM

NOTES & OTHER JAZZ

DAY ○

THE DAY'S #1 GOAL

3 TASKS THAT WILL HELP ME REACH MY GOAL

1.
2.
3.

EVENING ☾

HOW WELL DID I ACCOMPLISH MY GOAL TODAY?

FAILURE ○ ○ ○ ○ ○ ○ ○ ○ ○ ○ SUCCESS!
         1 2 3 4 5 6 7 8 9 10

HERE'S A LITTLE SOMETHING I LEARNED TODAY

TODAY'S WINS

3 THINGS I'M THANKFUL FOR THIS EVENING

1.
2.
3.

DATE: / /   S M T W TH F S

Time	
5 AM	
6 AM	
7 AM	
8 AM	
9 AM	
10 AM	
11 AM	
12 PM	
1 PM	
2 PM	
3 PM	
4 PM	
5 PM	
6 PM	
7 PM	
8 PM	
9 PM	
10 PM	
11 PM	

NOTES & OTHER JAZZ

DAY ○

THE DAY'S #1 GOAL

3 TASKS THAT WILL HELP ME REACH MY GOAL

1.
2.
3.

EVENING ☾

HOW WELL DID I ACCOMPLISH MY GOAL TODAY?

FAILURE ○ ○ ○ ○ ○ ○ ○ ○ ○ ○ SUCCESS!
         1 2 3 4 5 6 7 8 9 10

HERE'S A LITTLE SOMETHING I LEARNED TODAY

TODAY'S WINS

3 THINGS I'M THANKFUL FOR THIS EVENING

1.
2.
3.

DATE: / /					S M T W TH F S

Time	
5 AM	
6 AM	
7 AM	
8 AM	
9 AM	
10 AM	
11 AM	
12 PM	
1 PM	
2 PM	
3 PM	
4 PM	
5 PM	
6 PM	
7 PM	
8 PM	
9 PM	
10 PM	
11 PM	

NOTES & OTHER JAZZ

DAY ○

THE DAY'S #1 GOAL

3 TASKS THAT WILL HELP ME REACH MY GOAL

1.
2.
3.

EVENING ☾

HOW WELL DID I ACCOMPLISH MY GOAL TODAY?

FAILURE ○ ○ ○ ○ ○ ○ ○ ○ ○ ○ SUCCESS!
　　　　 1 2 3 4 5 6 7 8 9 10

HERE'S A LITTLE SOMETHING I LEARNED TODAY

TODAY'S WINS

3 THINGS I'M THANKFUL FOR THIS EVENING

1.
2.
3.

DATE: / /   S M T W TH F S

5 AM
6 AM
7 AM
8 AM
9 AM
10 AM
11 AM
12 PM
1 PM
2 PM
3 PM
4 PM
5 PM
6 PM
7 PM
8 PM
9 PM
10 PM
11 PM

NOTES & OTHER JAZZ

DAY ○

THE DAY'S #1 GOAL

3 TASKS THAT WILL HELP ME REACH MY GOAL

1.
2.
3.

EVENING ☾

HOW WELL DID I ACCOMPLISH MY GOAL TODAY?

FAILURE ○ 1 ○ 2 ○ 3 ○ 4 ○ 5 ○ 6 ○ 7 ○ 8 ○ 9 ○ 10 SUCCESS!

HERE'S A LITTLE SOMETHING I LEARNED TODAY

TODAY'S WINS

3 THINGS I'M THANKFUL FOR THIS EVENING

1.
2.
3.

DATE: /   /   S M T W TH F S

Time	
5 AM	
6 AM	
7 AM	
8 AM	
9 AM	
10 AM	
11 AM	
12 PM	
1 PM	
2 PM	
3 PM	
4 PM	
5 PM	
6 PM	
7 PM	
8 PM	
9 PM	
10 PM	
11 PM	

NOTES & OTHER JAZZ

DAY ○

THE DAY'S #1 GOAL

3 TASKS THAT WILL HELP ME REACH MY GOAL

1.
2.
3.

EVENING ☾

HOW WELL DID I ACCOMPLISH MY GOAL TODAY?

FAILURE ○ 1 ○ 2 ○ 3 ○ 4 ○ 5 ○ 6 ○ 7 ○ 8 ○ 9 ○ 10 SUCCESS!

HERE'S A LITTLE SOMETHING I LEARNED TODAY

TODAY'S WINS

3 THINGS I'M THANKFUL FOR THIS EVENING

1.
2.
3.

DATE: /   /   S M T W TH F S

5 AM
6 AM
7 AM
8 AM
9 AM
10 AM
11 AM
12 PM
1 PM
2 PM
3 PM
4 PM
5 PM
6 PM
7 PM
8 PM
9 PM
10 PM
11 PM

NOTES & OTHER JAZZ

DAY ○

THE DAY'S #1 GOAL

3 TASKS THAT WILL HELP ME REACH MY GOAL

1.
2.
3.

EVENING

HOW WELL DID I ACCOMPLISH MY GOAL TODAY?

FAILURE ○ ○ ○ ○ ○ ○ ○ ○ ○ ○ SUCCESS!
       1   2   3   4   5   6   7   8   9   10

HERE'S A LITTLE SOMETHING I LEARNED TODAY

TODAY'S WINS

3 THINGS I'M THANKFUL FOR THIS EVENING

1.
2.
3.

DATE: / /   S M T W TH F S

5 AM
6 AM
7 AM
8 AM
9 AM
10 AM
11 AM
12 PM
1 PM
2 PM
3 PM
4 PM
5 PM
6 PM
7 PM
8 PM
9 PM
10 PM
11 PM

NOTES & OTHER JAZZ

DAY ○

THE DAY'S #1 GOAL

3 TASKS THAT WILL HELP ME REACH MY GOAL

1.
2.
3.

EVENING ☾

HOW WELL DID I ACCOMPLISH MY GOAL TODAY?

FAILURE ○ 1 ○ 2 ○ 3 ○ 4 ○ 5 ○ 6 ○ 7 ○ 8 ○ 9 ○ 10 SUCCESS!

HERE'S A LITTLE SOMETHING I LEARNED TODAY

TODAY'S WINS

3 THINGS I'M THANKFUL FOR THIS EVENING

1.
2.
3.

DATE: /   /   S M T W TH F S

Time		NOTES & OTHER JAZZ
5 AM		
6 AM		
7 AM		
8 AM		
9 AM		
10 AM		
11 AM		
12 PM		
1 PM		
2 PM		
3 PM		
4 PM		
5 PM		
6 PM		
7 PM		
8 PM		
9 PM		
10 PM		
11 PM		

DAY ○

THE DAY'S #1 GOAL

3 TASKS THAT WILL HELP ME REACH MY GOAL

1.
2.
3.

EVENING ☾

HOW WELL DID I ACCOMPLISH MY GOAL TODAY?

FAILURE ○ 1 ○ 2 ○ 3 ○ 4 ○ 5 ○ 6 ○ 7 ○ 8 ○ 9 ○ 10 SUCCESS!

HERE'S A LITTLE SOMETHING I LEARNED TODAY

TODAY'S WINS

3 THINGS I'M THANKFUL FOR THIS EVENING

1.
2.
3.

DATE: / /   S M T W TH F S

5 AM
6 AM
7 AM
8 AM
9 AM
10 AM
11 AM
12 PM
1 PM
2 PM
3 PM
4 PM
5 PM
6 PM
7 PM
8 PM
9 PM
10 PM
11 PM

NOTES & OTHER JAZZ

DAY ○

THE DAY'S #1 GOAL

3 TASKS THAT WILL HELP ME REACH MY GOAL

1.
2.
3.

EVENING ☾

HOW WELL DID I ACCOMPLISH MY GOAL TODAY?

FAILURE ○ ○ ○ ○ ○ ○ ○ ○ ○ ○ SUCCESS!
       1 2 3 4 5 6 7 8 9 10

HERE'S A LITTLE SOMETHING I LEARNED TODAY

TODAY'S WINS

3 THINGS I'M THANKFUL FOR THIS EVENING

1.
2.
3.

DATE: / /   S M T W TH F S

5 AM
6 AM
7 AM
8 AM
9 AM
10 AM
11 AM
12 PM
1 PM
2 PM
3 PM
4 PM
5 PM
6 PM
7 PM
8 PM
9 PM
10 PM
11 PM

NOTES & OTHER JAZZ

DAY 〇

THE DAY'S #1 GOAL

3 TASKS THAT WILL HELP ME REACH MY GOAL

1.
2.
3.

EVENING ☾

HOW WELL DID I ACCOMPLISH MY GOAL TODAY?

FAILURE 〇 〇 〇 〇 〇 〇 〇 〇 〇 〇 SUCCESS!
         1 2 3 4 5 6 7 8 9 10

HERE'S A LITTLE SOMETHING I LEARNED TODAY

TODAY'S WINS

3 THINGS I'M THANKFUL FOR THIS EVENING

1.
2.
3.

DATE: /   /   S M T W TH F S

5 AM
6 AM
7 AM
8 AM
9 AM
10 AM
11 AM
12 PM
1 PM
2 PM
3 PM
4 PM
5 PM
6 PM
7 PM
8 PM
9 PM
10 PM
11 PM

NOTES & OTHER JAZZ

DAY ○

THE DAY'S #1 GOAL

3 TASKS THAT WILL HELP ME REACH MY GOAL

1.
2.
3.

EVENING ☾

HOW WELL DID I ACCOMPLISH MY GOAL TODAY?

FAILURE ○ ○ ○ ○ ○ ○ ○ ○ ○ ○ SUCCESS!
       1 2 3 4 5 6 7 8 9 10

HERE'S A LITTLE SOMETHING I LEARNED TODAY

TODAY'S WINS

3 THINGS I'M THANKFUL FOR THIS EVENING

1.
2.
3.

DATE: / /   S M T W TH F S

5 AM
6 AM
7 AM
8 AM
9 AM
10 AM
11 AM
12 PM
1 PM
2 PM
3 PM
4 PM
5 PM
6 PM
7 PM
8 PM
9 PM
10 PM
11 PM

NOTES & OTHER JAZZ

DAY ○

THE DAY'S #1 GOAL

3 TASKS THAT WILL HELP ME REACH MY GOAL

1.
2.
3.

EVENING ☾

HOW WELL DID I ACCOMPLISH MY GOAL TODAY?

FAILURE ○ ○ ○ ○ ○ ○ ○ ○ ○ ○ SUCCESS!
       1 2 3 4 5 6 7 8 9 10

HERE'S A LITTLE SOMETHING I LEARNED TODAY

TODAY'S WINS

3 THINGS I'M THANKFUL FOR THIS EVENING

1.
2.
3.

DATE: / /   S M T W TH F S

- 5 AM
- 6 AM
- 7 AM
- 8 AM
- 9 AM
- 10 AM
- 11 AM
- 12 PM
- 1 PM
- 2 PM
- 3 PM
- 4 PM
- 5 PM
- 6 PM
- 7 PM
- 8 PM
- 9 PM
- 10 PM
- 11 PM

NOTES & OTHER JAZZ

DAY ○

THE DAY'S #1 GOAL

3 TASKS THAT WILL HELP ME REACH MY GOAL

1.
2.
3.

EVENING ☾

HOW WELL DID I ACCOMPLISH MY GOAL TODAY?

FAILURE ○ 1 ○ 2 ○ 3 ○ 4 ○ 5 ○ 6 ○ 7 ○ 8 ○ 9 ○ 10 SUCCESS!

HERE'S A LITTLE SOMETHING I LEARNED TODAY

TODAY'S WINS

3 THINGS I'M THANKFUL FOR THIS EVENING

1.
2.
3.

DATE: /   /   S M T W TH F S

5 AM
6 AM
7 AM
8 AM
9 AM
10 AM
11 AM
12 PM
1 PM
2 PM
3 PM
4 PM
5 PM
6 PM
7 PM
8 PM
9 PM
10 PM
11 PM

NOTES & OTHER JAZZ

DAY 〇

THE DAY'S #1 GOAL

3 TASKS THAT WILL HELP ME REACH MY GOAL

1.
2.
3.

EVENING ☾

HOW WELL DID I ACCOMPLISH MY GOAL TODAY?

FAILURE ○ 1 ○ 2 ○ 3 ○ 4 ○ 5 ○ 6 ○ 7 ○ 8 ○ 9 ○ 10 SUCCESS!

HERE'S A LITTLE SOMETHING I LEARNED TODAY

TODAY'S WINS

3 THINGS I'M THANKFUL FOR THIS EVENING

1.
2.
3.

DATE: /   /   S M T W TH F S

Time		NOTES & OTHER JAZZ
5 AM		
6 AM		
7 AM		
8 AM		
9 AM		
10 AM		
11 AM		
12 PM		
1 PM		
2 PM		
3 PM		
4 PM		
5 PM		
6 PM		
7 PM		
8 PM		
9 PM		
10 PM		
11 PM		

DAY ○

THE DAY'S #1 GOAL

3 TASKS THAT WILL HELP ME REACH MY GOAL

1.
2.
3.

EVENING ☾

HOW WELL DID I ACCOMPLISH MY GOAL TODAY?

FAILURE ○ ○ ○ ○ ○ ○ ○ ○ ○ ○ SUCCESS!
       1   2   3   4   5   6   7   8   9   10

HERE'S A LITTLE SOMETHING I LEARNED TODAY

TODAY'S WINS

3 THINGS I'M THANKFUL FOR THIS EVENING

1.
2.
3.

DATE: / /   S M T W TH F S

5 AM
6 AM
7 AM
8 AM
9 AM
10 AM
11 AM
12 PM
1 PM
2 PM
3 PM
4 PM
5 PM
6 PM
7 PM
8 PM
9 PM
10 PM
11 PM

NOTES & OTHER JAZZ

DAY ○

THE DAY'S #1 GOAL

3 TASKS THAT WILL HELP ME REACH MY GOAL

1.
2.
3.

EVENING ☾

HOW WELL DID I ACCOMPLISH MY GOAL TODAY?

FAILURE ○ ○ ○ ○ ○ ○ ○ ○ ○ ○ SUCCESS!
         1 2 3 4 5 6 7 8 9 10

HERE'S A LITTLE SOMETHING I LEARNED TODAY

TODAY'S WINS

3 THINGS I'M THANKFUL FOR THIS EVENING

1.
2.
3.

Copyright © 2019, Bucko Book Co. All rights reserved. This book or any portion thereof may not be reproduced or used in any manner whatsoever without the express written permission of the publisher except for the use of brief quotations in a book review.

ISBN: 9781794373136

Made in the USA
Coppell, TX
30 December 2019